Mysterious Places Around the World

Exploring Earth's Enigmas

Ashraf Almamlouk

Title: Tales from the Jungle: Courage .. Confidence .. Kindness
Written and Illustrated by: Ashraf Almamlouk
Published by: Draft2Digital

"To the explorers, dreamers, and seekers of the unknown. May your curiosity lead you to uncharted places, and your discoveries inspire the world."

"Man cannot discover new oceans unless he has the courage to lose sight of the shore."
– André Gide

CONTENT

Introduction

The Allure of the Unknown

Throughout human history, we have been captivated by the mysterious and the unexplained. From ancient ruins shrouded in legend to natural wonders that defy conventional understanding, our Earth is home to countless enigmatic locations that continue to intrigue and inspire us. These mysterious places around the world serve as a testament to the enduring power of the unknown to capture our collective imagination.

Why are we so drawn to these perplexing sites? Perhaps it's the thrill of unraveling age-old mysteries, or the excitement of contemplating alternative explanations for the seemingly inexplicable. Whatever the reason, mysterious places have a unique ability to awaken our sense of wonder and curiosity about the world around us.

In this book, we will embark on a journey to explore some of Earth's most captivating enigmas. From the ancient wonders of Egypt to the mist-shrouded mountains of Peru, we'll delve into the histories, theories, and ongoing investigations surrounding these fascinating locations. Our exploration will include many locations with unsolved mysteries that continue to baffle experts with their precise construction and alignment, such as the Pyramids of Giza, Stonehenge, Easter Island.

As we examine these and other mysterious places, we'll consider various theories proposed by archaeologists, historians, and other researchers.

Ashraf Almamlouk

Chapter 1

Ancient Mysteries

The Pyramids of Giza

Introduction

The Pyramids of Giza stand as silent sentinels, their immense forms dominating the landscape for millennia. These magnificent structures, testaments to ancient Egyptian ingenuity, have captivated humanity for centuries, sparking endless debate and speculation on their construction. How did a civilization, thousands of years ago, manage to erect such colossal monuments without the benefit of modern technology? The answer remains elusive, but countless theories and hypotheses attempt to unravel the enigma of their creation.

Imagine a building so vast, so complex, and so meticulously crafted that it takes thousands of workers decades to complete. Is it truly believable that its sole purpose was simply to house a single, deceased ruler? This is the question that has puzzled historians, archaeologists, and curious minds for centuries.

The sheer scale of the Pyramids is staggering. The Great Pyramid of Khufu, the largest of the three, is a masterpiece of engineering, composed of an estimated 2.3 million blocks of stone, each weighing an average of 2.5 tons. To put this into perspective, it's like lifting and placing over 6 million cars! This monumental task, executed with remarkable precision, leads us to question the methods employed by the ancient Egyptians.

The Kings' Tombs

The Tomb Theory:

There are a number of theories and hypotheses about the purpose the pyramids were intended to serve. The most widely accepted theory is that the pyramids were built as tombs for the pharaohs of Ancient Egypt and their consorts during the Old Kingdom.

It's believed that the pyramid was seen as a means for the pharaoh to ascend to the sky and become godlike. The pyramid was viewed as a place for the pharaoh's final journey in the solar barque. The Egyptian word for pyramid, myr, literally means "place of ascension." The smooth exterior of the pyramid would also symbolize the rays of the sun and the pharaoh's role as the "living sun god" Ra.

The elaborate design: The intricate passageways, chambers, and hidden rooms were clearly designed with a purpose in mind, and many believe that purpose was to protect the pharaoh's body and belongings for eternity.

The symbolic connection to the afterlife: Ancient Egyptian beliefs placed great emphasis on the journey to the afterlife. The pyramids, with their precise alignment and celestial symbolism, could be seen as a way to ensure a safe passage for the pharaoh's soul.

Challenging the Tomb Theory:

While the tomb theory is widely accepted, it doesn't fully explain all the mysteries surrounding the pyramids. Several questions and alternative hypotheses have been put forward:

The massive scale and excess: If the sole purpose was burial, why were these structures built on such a monumental scale, with far more resources than would seem necessary?

The complex ventilation and engineering: The pyramids are incredibly well-ventilated, even featuring shafts that seem to point towards specific stars. Was this truly necessary for a tomb, or could there be another, more sophisticated reason for their design?

The hidden chambers and cryptic symbols: The discovery of hidden chambers and strange symbols within the pyramids has fuelled speculation about secret knowledge and rituals that may have been practiced there.

The astronomical alignment: The pyramids are remarkably aligned with celestial bodies. Could this indicate a deeper connection to astronomy, perhaps used for studying the stars or marking significant celestial events?

Alignments and Angles:

Whispers of a Celestial Plan

One of the most compelling pieces of evidence supporting the astronomical theory is the meticulous alignment of the pyramids with the cardinal directions – north, south, east, and west. Archaeologists and astronomers have observed that the pyramids, particularly the Great Pyramid of Giza, are remarkably aligned with the true north, with an accuracy that is astonishing for a structure built thousands of years ago. This precise orientation suggests a deliberate attempt to connect the earthly realm with the celestial sphere, allowing the pyramids to serve as markers for astronomical events.

Furthermore, the internal passages and chambers within the pyramids seem to be strategically placed to align with specific stars and constellations at particular times of the year. For instance, the descending passage of the Great Pyramid appears to be aligned with the star Thuban, which was the North Star during the time the pyramid was built. Similarly, some researchers suggest that the air shafts within the pyramid were designed to frame specific stars visible at sunrise and sunset during significant events on the Egyptian calendar.

The Geometry of Power

The very design of the pyramids hints at a deeper purpose. The precise angles, the meticulous placement of stones, and the intricate internal chambers seem to defy mere architectural whims. Some believe that the shape itself, a pyramid, was chosen for its unique ability to interact with energies found in the environment. Imagine a giant antenna, designed to capture and focus certain types of energy – could the pyramids have served this role?

Consider the concept of scalar energy. Some scientists believe that the pyramids, with their geometric form and specific orientation, could have acted as resonators, capable of manipulating these unseen energies. This theory suggests that the pyramids weren't just built to impress, but to harness a fundamental force of nature.

The Secrets of Granite and Quartz:

The materials used in the pyramids are another piece of the puzzle. Granite, a crystalline rock, and quartz, known for its piezoelectric properties, are abundant in the structures. Piezoelectricity is the ability of certain materials to generate an electrical charge in response to mechanical stress, like pressure or vibration. Could the immense weight of the pyramid stones, coupled with the earth's natural vibrations, have created an electrical current?

Some researchers propose that the pyramids acted as giant crystal oscillators. The precise arrangement of granite and quartz could have created a network that amplified natural vibrations, leading to the generation of significant energy. This energy, some believe, could have been used for various purposes, from powering light sources to influencing the environment.

The Cosmic Connection:

The pyramids are also intricately linked to the cosmos. Their alignment with the stars and constellations suggests a deep understanding of astronomy and celestial cycles. Could this alignment have been more than just a symbolic gesture? Perhaps it was a crucial element in the pyramid's supposed energy generating capacity.

Some researchers believe that the pyramids were designed to harness cosmic rays or other forms of energy emanating from the universe. This 'cosmic energy' could have been captured and channeled through the pyramid's structure, amplified by the geometric design and materials. It's a fascinating idea that connects the pyramids to the vast expanse of the universe.

Now, let's delve into the fascinating theories and hypotheses surrounding the possibility of advanced technology hidden within the Pyramids.

Ramp and Lever Power:

The most widely accepted theory proposes that the Pyramids were built using a combination of ramps and levers. Imagine a vast network of ramps, gradually inclining towards the pyramid's peak. These ramps, possibly constructed of earth, brick, or stone, would have provided a pathway for hauling the massive stone blocks. Workers, likely a large workforce of skilled laborers and craftsmen, would have used levers, rollers, and ropes to maneuver the blocks along the ramps, eventually positioning them into place.

This hypothesis is supported by evidence found at Giza, including remnants of possible ramp systems and ancient tools. However, the exact configuration of these ramps remains a subject of debate. The sheer length and steepness of the ramps required to reach the upper levels pose logistical challenges, especially considering the weight of the gigantic stones.

Water, Wood, and the Nile's Contribution:

Another hypothesis focuses on the role of the Nile River and the plentiful supply of wood available during that time. The theory suggests that the stone blocks were transported by water, utilizing barges and boats to navigate the river to the construction site. Once near the pyramid, the blocks could have been lifted onto smaller boats and subsequently onto ramps using a system of levers and rollers.

This theory is supported by the proximity of the Nile to the Giza plateau. The abundance of wood, a key resource for building boats, rafts, and temporary structures, would have been invaluable for the construction process. However, the exact methods for transporting such massive blocks, especially towards the higher levels, still remain unclear.

The Acoustic Secrets of the Pyramids:

Traditionally, the conventional narrative of pyramid construction focuses on brute force, the herculean efforts of thousands of laborers hauling massive stones into place. But what if there was another force at play, a hidden element that guided the hands of the builders and shaped the very essence of these monumental structures? What if sound, specifically acoustic principles, played a pivotal role in their design and construction?

The hypothesis that sound played a crucial role in pyramid construction is based on a fascinating concept known as "cymatics." Cymatics is the study of visible sound, exploring how sound waves create intricate patterns in various mediums like sand, water, and even air.

Some theorists postulate that the ancient Egyptians might have understood this principle and used it to manipulate the very building blocks of the pyramids. By producing specific sound frequencies, they could have potentially levitated or guided the massive stone blocks into place with greater ease and precision.

While this idea might sound fantastical, it's grounded in scientific principles. We know that sound waves possess energy and can exert pressure on objects. It's not entirely inconceivable that a sufficiently powerful and focused sound wave could influence the movement of heavy objects.

While we may never know the exact methods used to build the pyramids, the idea that sound played a role opens a remarkable window into ancient Egyptian ingenuity. Modern construction techniques still recognize the power of rhythm and sound in labor. For instance, teams today might also use music to increase productivity and morale.

Gravity: A Force Beyond Our Understanding?

One such intriguing field of exploration focuses on gravity – the invisible force that binds us to the Earth. We all experience its effects every day, but its true nature remains shrouded in mystery. Modern physics, with Einstein's theory of general relativity, paints a picture of gravity as a warping of spacetime, a force that curves the very fabric of reality. But could our ancestors have possessed a deeper understanding of this force, a knowledge that enabled them to manipulate it in ways we can only dream of?

Some theorists propose that the ancient Egyptians, through a profound understanding of cosmic energies and resonance, discovered subtle ways to influence gravity. This is often linked to the concept of "zero-point energy," a hypothetical energy inherent in the quantum vacuum of space. By harnessing this energy, they might have been able to reduce the effective weight of the massive stone blocks, making them easier to move and position.

The traditional narrative, while dominant, faces a barrage of questions that have fueled the flames of alternative explanations. How did a civilization, seemingly emerging from relative obscurity, achieve such a feat of engineering? Moving colossal stones, precisely shaping them, and assembling them with millimetre precision demands a level of technological prowess rarely seen in other ancient societies.

Furthermore, the pyramids themselves seem to hold an uncanny alignment with celestial bodies, suggesting a profound understanding of astronomy far beyond what is commonly attributed to the ancient Egyptians. The precise orientation of the Great Pyramid towards true north, the ventilation shafts aligning with specific stars, and the intricate geometry woven into the structure all point towards a level of sophistication that raises eyebrows among skeptics and fuels the imaginations of those open to alternative possibilities.

One of the most prominent theories posits that extraterrestrial visitors played a pivotal role in the construction of the pyramids. Perhaps, they were benevolent guides, sharing their advanced knowledge with the ancient Egyptians, fostering a technological leap that propelled civilization into an unprecedented era of architectural prowess.

This hypothesis gains traction from the seemingly inexplicable engineering feats encapsulated in the pyramids. The precision of the stonework, the use of sophisticated mathematical principles, and the evidence of advanced understanding of astronomy all suggest a guiding hand from a source beyond human comprehension at that time. Could the intricate symbolism found within the pyramids be a form of communication, a message left behind by our interstellar visitors?

Conclusion

The Pyramids of Giza continue to astound and confound researchers, historians, and enthusiasts alike. While many theories have been proposed to explain their purpose and construction, the truth remains elusive. As new archaeological discoveries emerge and technologies advance, our understanding of these majestic structures may evolve. For now, the pyramids stand as a testament to human ingenuity, a link to a rich cultural past, and an enduring mystery that invites exploration and wonder. Whether as tombs, astronomical observatories, or something beyond our current understanding, the pyramids of Giza will forever be a source of intrigue and fascination.

Stonehenge, England

Introduction

In the rolling hills of Wiltshire, England, lies one of the most enigmatic and fascinating archaeological sites in the world - Stonehenge. For centuries, this prehistoric monument has captivated the imagination of scholars, tourists, and the general public alike. Its towering stones and intricate ring formations tell a story steeped in mystery, leading to a plethora of theories about its origins, purpose, and significance.

In this book, we will delve into the world of Stonehenge, uncovering its history, exploring the various myths and legends that surround it, and examining the theories that have been proposed to explain this ancient wonder. From its possible astronomical connections to its potential use as a burial site for high-ranking individuals, we will explore all aspects of this iconic English landmark.

History of Stonehenge

Stonehenge's history stretches back over 5000 years, with the construction of the site taking place in several stages. The first phase, which began around 3000 BC, saw the creation of a henge (a circular ditch and bank enclosure) around which numerous wooden posts were erected. These posts were later replaced by the iconic standing stones we see today, with the largest stones, known as the sarsens, being brought from quarries over 100 miles away in Wales.

The second stage of construction began around 2500 BC, with the addition of a circle of smaller, more uniform stones known as the bluestones. These stones were also transported from Wales, with the exact path of their journey still unknown. This phase also saw the creation of a series of earthworks and burial mounds surrounding the main site.

The final phase of construction took place around 1500 BC, with the arrangement of the sarsens into the iconic horseshoe and circle shape we see today. Further modifications were made over the centuries, with the last recorded changes taking place during the Roman era.

Myths and Legends

Stonehenge has been the subject of numerous myths and legends throughout history, each attempting to explain the origins and purpose of this mysterious site. One of the earliest stories explains Stonehenge as the work of giants. These powerful beings, some say, were responsible for lifting these enormous stones, placing them with superhuman strength, and creating a magical circle of power. Some legends even tell of a magician named Merlin, a powerful magician from Arthurian tales, who supposedly moved the stones from Ireland to Salisbury Plain using his magic.

The Merlin Mystery and the Giants' Dance:

Stonehenge also features in the legends of King Arthur and the Knights of the Round Table. One of the most famous stories is that of Merlin the magician, who is said to have magically transported the stones from Ireland to England. According to the legend, the stones were originally part of a circle in Ireland known as the Giant's Ring. Merlin, at the request of King Arthur, used his magical powers to move the stones to Salisbury Plain, where they were erected as a memorial to the fallen warriors of a great battle. This legend not only ties Stonehenge to the Arthurian mythos but also adds a sense of wonder and enchantment to the monument.

Though this story is likely a blend of folklore and imagination, it speaks to the human desire to understand the origins of something so magnificent. The idea of a powerful magician wielding his magic to create this awe-inspiring monument adds a layer of wonder to the already mysterious history of Stonehenge.

Another popular myth tells of the stones themselves being magical. They were believed to have the power to heal, to predict the future, and to communicate with the spirits of the dead. Some stories even suggest that the stones were a gateway to another world, allowing those who approached them to communicate with gods or other powerful beings.

The Sun's Dance and the Cycle of Life:

Stonehenge's alignment with the sun and moon has fueled many beliefs and rituals. The ancient builders, it is believed, carefully placed the stones to mark the solstices and equinoxes – the longest and shortest days of the year, and the days when the hours of daylight and night are equal.

This connection to the sun and its cycles led to the belief that Stonehenge was a sacred site for worshipping the sun god. Many myths suggest that the stones were used as a giant calendar, a way to track the seasons and predict the future. People gathered at Stonehenge during these special times, offering prayers and sacrifices to ensure good harvests and a prosperous year.

This focus on the celestial bodies and the passage of time led to the belief that Stonehenge was a place of life, death, and rebirth. Some myths tell of the stones being a burial ground for kings and heroes, a final resting place where they could connect with the sun's energy and continue their journey to the afterlife.

Druids and Whispers of the Past:

Another popular legend connects Stonehenge with the ancient Druids, the priestly class of the Celtic people. According to this myth, the Druids used Stonehenge as a sacred site for their religious ceremonies and rituals. It is said that they performed human sacrifices, initiations, and other important rites at the monument.

The alignment of the stones with the solstices and equinoxes is often cited as evidence of the Druids' advanced knowledge of astronomy and their use of Stonehenge as an astronomical calendar. This legend not only adds a layer of mysticism to Stonehenge but also emphasizes its role as a center of spiritual and cultural significance.

The Curse of Stonehenge:

Another intriguing legend is the curse associated with Stonehenge. According to this myth, anyone who attempts to tamper with or remove the stones from their original positions will suffer a terrible fate. This curse is said to protect the monument from harm and ensure that its secrets remain hidden. The legend serves as a warning to those who might be tempted to exploit or vandalize the site, emphasizing the sacred and inviolable nature of Stonehenge.

Conclusion

Today, Stonehenge is a UNESCO World Heritage Site, a place that draws visitors from all over the world. Standing among the stones, you can feel the weight of history, the whispers of the past. It's a place that sparks wonder and curiosity, and reminds us that long before us, people were looking up at the same sky, wondering about the universe and their place within it.

Stonehenge is a reminder that the past is not just a collection of facts and figures. It is a story, filled with mysteries and enigmas that continue to inspire us. It's a testament to the ingenuity and imagination of people who lived thousands of years ago, and a window into the ancient world that continues to inspire awe and wonder.

Even though we may never fully understand the meaning of Stonehenge, it remains a powerful symbol of our shared human experience. Its enduring mystery keeps its story alive, a constant reminder that there are still many secrets hidden within the earth, waiting to be discovered.

Easter Island

Introduction

Easter Island, a remote speck of land in the vast expanse of the Pacific Ocean, has captivated the imaginations of explorers, scientists, and enthusiasts for centuries. This small, volcanic island, officially known as Rapa Nui, is shrouded in mystery, most notably due to its iconic moai, the colossal stone statues that dot the landscape. But the enigma of Easter Island extends far beyond its statues; it encompasses a unique culture, a complex history, and a fascinating ecological collapse, all unfolding in a seemingly isolated corner of the world. This book delves into the prevailing theories surrounding the island's mysteries, exploring the origins of its inhabitants, the construction of the moai, and the factors that led to its dramatic societal decline.

Long ago, before the arrival of Europeans, the island thrived with a rich culture. The Polynesians, skilled navigators and seafarers, likely from the Marquesas Islands, sometime between 800 and 1200 AD, sailed across the ocean to settle on the sun-drenched shores of Easter Island. They brought with them stories of their ancestors and gods, woven into the fabric of their daily lives. It was here that the myths and legends began to take shape.

Among the most striking features of Easter Island are the moai—enormous stone statues carved from volcanic rock. These majestic figures stand silently, their stone gazes watching over the island and its people. It is said that each moai represents an important ancestor, embodying their spirit and ensuring the prosperity of the community. But who built them? Why are they so numerous? And what stories do they hold?

The Moai

Stone Guardians of the Past:

The moai are the undisputed stars of Easter Island. Carved from volcanic rock, these colossal statues range in size from a few feet to over 30 feet tall and weigh several tons. Their origins are one of the greatest mysteries surrounding the island.

How did the islanders, with seemingly limited technology, manage to transport these massive stones across the island? Did they use wooden rollers, ramps, or perhaps even ropes and sleds? Archaeologists and scientists have been debating these questions for years, proposing various theories and conducting experiments to try and understand the engineering feat behind the moai's movement. Some even believe the moai were walked across the island using a specific technique!

The 'Ramp' Theory:

This prevailing theory suggests that the moai were carved from volcanic rock and transported using ramps and levers. Evidence of ramps and pathways near the quarries and statue platforms supports this theory.

The 'Rolling' Theory:

Another theory proposes that the moai were moved by tilting and rolling them on wooden rollers or sleds. This theory is supported by the fact that the moai are relatively narrow and could potentially be moved in this manner.

The 'Walking' Theory:

A more recent and controversial theory suggests that the moai were moved by a "walking" technique, potentially with ropes and logs. This theory gained traction after experiments showed that it was possible to move large, heavy objects using this method.

While the purpose of the moai remains unclear, theories abound. Some believe they were representations of ancestors or chiefs, symbols of power and status. Others suggest they were linked to spiritual beliefs, acting as protectors and guardians of the land. The moai's placement across the island, often facing inland towards the villages, adds to the intrigue.

A Society in Decline

The Rongorongo Script:

The early Rapa Nui society was a fascinating blend of tradition and innovation. They developed a complex system of agriculture, cultivating sweet potatoes and other crops to sustain themselves. They also created a unique writing system called Rongorongo.

Rongorongo is a fascinating example of a unique script found in Polynesia. It's carved onto wooden tablets, mainly made from the wood of the extinct toromiro tree. Unfortunately, the meaning of this script has remained a mystery, despite extensive efforts by scholars to decipher it. Few tablets have been found and most of them are damaged. Only a handful of experts are able to identify individual glyphs and symbols.

The mystery of Rongorongo is heartbreaking. It's a lost piece of the Rapa Nui puzzle, a potential key to unlocking their history, culture, and beliefs. Imagine the stories, the legends, and the knowledge that could be unlocked if we understood what these symbols represent!

The Ecological Collapse and Societal Decline:

The story of Easter Island also serves as a cautionary tale about the fragility of island ecosystems and the consequences of unsustainable practices. Archaeological evidence suggests that the island experienced a significant environmental degradation, leading to deforestation, soil erosion, and a decline in biodiversity. This is believed to have been caused by a combination of factors, including population growth, unsustainable resource use, and possibly warfare.

Environmental Impact and Societal Collapse:

The ecological theories surrounding Easter Island's environmental degradation and the eventual decline of its civilization are both captivating and troubling. How did a thriving society filled with intricately constructed statues and vibrant culture fall to collapse?

Deforestation: Researchers, including archaeologists and ecologists, point to the clearing of trees to meet the demands of a growing population and the needs related to moai construction as a critical factor. The loss of trees would have affected the island's agricultural potential, leading to food shortages.

Resource Depletion: With the decline of the island's ecosystem came a struggle for survival. This resource depletion theory posits that intense competition and internal strife could have led to societal collapse, as rival factions clashed over dwindling resources.

Climate Change and Natural Disasters: Some scholars argue that external factors like climatic shifts, volcanic activity, and disease may have influenced the island's decline. Understanding how these external forces impacted the Rapa Nui civilization can provide a broader context for its challenges.

The Arrival of Europeans:

In 1722, the Dutch explorer Jacob Roggeveen became the first European to set foot on Easter Island. Sadly, the arrival of Europeans marked a further decline for the remaining Rapa Nui people. Diseases, slavery, and the introduction of foreign cultures had devastating consequences.

Unanswered Questions:

The mystery of Easter Island continues to fascinate scientists, historians, and archaeologists. While we have learned a great deal about the Rapa Nui people and their culture, many questions remain unanswered. Why were the moai abandoned? What caused the collapse of their society? What can we learn from the mistakes of the past?

Researchers are constantly exploring new theories, examining ancient artifacts, and using advanced technologies like DNA analysis and 3D modeling to piece together a richer understanding of this fascinating island.

Conclusion

Easter Island serves as a potent reminder of the delicate balance between humanity and the environment, and the importance of sustainable living. It's a place where the past whispers secrets, a place of incredible beauty and enduring mystery. The story of Rapa Nui, a story of resilience and adaptation, is a powerful lesson for us all.

Machu Picchu

Introduction

Nestled high in the Peruvian Andes, Machu Picchu stands as a testament to the ingenuity and artistry of the Inca civilization. This ancient city, shrouded in mist and teeming with intrigue, has captivated the world since its rediscovery in 1911. While its breathtaking beauty is undeniable, the true purpose and significance of Machu Picchu remain shrouded in mystery. This book delves into the various theories that attempt to unravel the enigmatic secrets of this lost city of the Incas.

The Royal Estate Theory:

Perhaps the most widely accepted theory posits that Machu Picchu was a royal estate, a secluded retreat for the Inca elite. Evidence for this theory includes the presence of luxurious residences, including the famed

"Royal Tomb," along with sophisticated agricultural terraces and a complex water management system. Historians suggest that it might have been a sanctuary for Inca royalty, allowing them to escape the bustling capital of Cusco and enjoy a serene environment. This theory further suggests that Machu Picchu could have been a place of spiritual and political significance, where the Inca rulers could connect with the divine and solidify their power.

The Religious Sanctuary Theory:

Another prominent theory proposes that Machu Picchu was a sacred religious site, a place of worship dedicated to the Inca deities. The presence of numerous temples, including the Temple of the Sun and the Intihuatana (Hitching Post of the Sun), lends credence to this idea. The location of the city, perched atop a mountain with stunning views, also hints at its possible significance in Inca cosmology. Certain scholars believe that Machu Picchu was a place where rituals and ceremonies were performed, connecting the Inca people with the spiritual realm and their ancestors. The intricate astronomical alignments of the city further reinforce this theory, suggesting a deep connection with the celestial bodies and a sophisticated understanding of astronomy.

The Military Fortress Theory:

Some researchers, however, lean towards a more pragmatic interpretation of Machu Picchu, suggesting its function as a strategic military fortress. The city's location, surrounded by towering mountains and difficult terrain, provided an ideal defense against potential invaders. The strategically placed walls, watchtowers, and narrow pathways could have aided in defending against enemy attacks. This theory gains further support from the discovery of various defensive structures within the city, including ingenious traps and hidden pathways. While not as widely accepted as the other theories, the military aspect of Machu Picchu cannot be completely ignored.

The Agricultural and Economic Hub Theory:

Machu Picchu's intricate agricultural terraces are a testament to the Inca's mastery of farming in challenging environments. Some historians believe that the city was primarily an agricultural and economic hub, a center for food production and resource management. The terraces allowed the Incas to cultivate diverse crops, ensuring a stable food supply for the population residing within the city and potentially also for Cusco. The presence of sophisticated water management systems further reinforces the idea of Machu Picchu as a self-sufficient agricultural center, crucial for the sustenance of the Inca empire.

The Enigma of the Abandoned City:

Irrespective of the specific purpose, one of the most intriguing aspects of Machu Picchu is its sudden abandonment. The city was seemingly deserted within a century of its construction, leaving behind a wealth of unanswered questions. Some scholars suggest that disease, war, or environmental factors might have led to the decline and eventual abandonment of the city. However, the lack of conclusive evidence makes it challenging to pinpoint the exact reasons for its desertion.

The Ongoing Research:

The mysteries surrounding Machu Picchu continue to fascinate archaeologists and historians. Ongoing research through archaeological excavations, technological advancements, and detailed analysis of existing structures are shedding new light on various aspects of the city. Future discoveries might reveal even more about the life and purpose of the Inca inhabitants, potentially leading to a better understanding of the complex societal and cultural fabric that shaped this extraordinary city.

Conclusion

The true purpose of Machu Picchu remains a captivating puzzle, a testament to the enduring fascination with the ingenuity and mystery of the Inca civilization. While each theory offers valuable insights, it is likely that the city served multiple functions, encompassing elements of royal residence, religious worship, agricultural management, and perhaps even strategic defense. As research progresses, we can expect further revelations that will hopefully shed light on the fascinating tapestry of this enigmatic city, helping us to better understand the whispers of the Andes and the legacy of the Incas.

Chapter 2

Natural Wonders

Bermuda Triangle

Introduction

The Bermuda Triangle, also known as the Devil's Triangle, a roughly triangular area in the North Atlantic Ocean bounded by Miami, Bermuda, and San Juan, has captivated the human imagination for decades. This infamous patch of water has been the subject of countless tales, legends, and theories, all centered around the baffling disappearances of ships and aircraft within its boundaries. While some dismiss the phenomenon as mere coincidence or sensationalized media hype, others cling to more extraordinary explanations, ranging from paranormal activity to advanced alien technology.

This exploration delves into the various theories and hypotheses surrounding the Bermuda Triangle, seeking to shed light on the possible causes behind these enigmatic disappearances.

The legend of the Bermuda Triangle originated in 1945, when Flight 19, a group of five U.S. Navy TBM Avenger torpedo bombers on a training mission, disappeared while flying over the area. All 14 airmen on the flight were never found or heard from again. This incident spawned a wave of speculation and sensationalized reporting, suggesting that supernatural forces, alien activity, or Atlantis was the cause.

Early Unexplained Disappearances The first reported incident was in 1944 when several U.S. Navy TBF Avenger torpedo bombers left Fort Lauderdale, Florida on a training mission but never returned. Further incidents include a DC-3 passenger plane carrying 33 people which took off from Puerto Rico and was never heard of again, and a flight of U.S. Marines where only a brief distress call was received before they disappeared.

One of the most intriguing early cases was the disappearance of the SS Marine Sulphur Queen, a tanker ship carrying a cargo of sulphur, in 1963. No distress call was sent and no wreckage was ever found. At 581 feet long, the Marine Sulphur Queen was one of the largest ships to vanish within the Triangle. Also, there have been many cases of aircraft disappearance and crashes within the Bermuda Triangle.

The Meteorological Perspective

Storms and Rogue Waves:

One of the most plausible explanations for the disappearances lies in the region's volatile weather patterns. The Bermuda Triangle is a frequent breeding ground for powerful hurricanes and tropical storms, whose unpredictable and destructive forces can easily overwhelm vessels and aircraft. The Gulf Stream, a strong and swift ocean current, further contributes to the region's instability, creating sudden and unpredictable changes in weather conditions.

Furthermore, the area is susceptible to the formation of rogue waves, exceptionally large and unpredictable waves that can appear suddenly and without warning. These colossal waves, capable of reaching heights of over 100 feet, can easily capsize even the most robust ships. The unpredictable nature of these waves, coupled with the region's frequent storms, makes navigation exceptionally challenging and hazardous.

The Geological Perspective

Methane Hydrate Outgassing and Underwater Volcanoes:

The ocean floor within the Bermuda Triangle holds numerous geological features that could potentially contribute to maritime disasters. One theory suggests that methane hydrate, a frozen form of methane found in the seabed, can destabilize and release vast quantities of gas into the water column. This sudden release can create large craters in the water, reducing buoyancy and potentially causing ships to sink rapidly.

Additionally, the area is known to have active underwater volcanoes. While volcanic eruptions are rare, they can cause significant disruptions to shipping lanes, creating unpredictable currents and releasing toxic gases that can be harmful to both humans and machinery. The unpredictable nature of these geological phenomena adds another layer of complexity to the challenges faced by vessels navigating the area.

The Human Error Factor

Navigation Mistakes and Mechanical Failures:

While speculative theories often dominate the conversation around the Bermuda Triangle, it's vital to acknowledge the role of human error in maritime accidents. The vastness of the ocean, coupled with the challenges of navigation, can lead to mistakes in charting courses, calculating distances, and interpreting weather patterns.

Furthermore, mechanical failures in vessels and aircraft can lead to catastrophic consequences, particularly in a region as geographically challenging and weather-prone as the Bermuda Triangle. The complexity of modern maritime and aviation technology, while offering many advantages, can also present unforeseen vulnerabilities, making vessels vulnerable to malfunction and potential disaster.

The Paranormal and Extraterrestrial Theories:

Despite the rational explanations offered by science, the allure of the paranormal persists. The unexplained nature of many disappearances, the lack of wreckage in some cases, and the sheer strangeness of some incidents have fueled speculation about more exotic explanations.

One popular theory involves the existence of a powerful magnetic anomaly in the region. Some believe that the Triangle's unique geological features might be disrupting compasses and navigation systems, potentially leading to disastrous results for passing vessels and aircraft. This theory, however, lacks substantial scientific evidence.

Then, there are the more fantastical theories, those that tread into the realms of science fiction. Some believe that the Triangle is a portal to another dimension, perhaps a gateway to a parallel universe or a hidden underwater civilization. Others suggest that extraterrestrial activity or ancient alien technology might be responsible for the disappearances. These ideas, while captivating, are based largely on speculation and lack credible evidence.

Debunking the Myths: Statistics and Reality

One of the key arguments against the paranormal theories is that the number of disappearances in the Bermuda Triangle isn't significantly higher than in other heavily trafficked maritime areas of the world. Statistics show that the number of accidents in this region is proportionate to the amount of sea and air travel that takes place there. The perception of increased risk is likely due to the concentration of media attention on this specific area.

Conclusion

The Bermuda Triangle continues to be a subject of fascination and debate. While scientific theories offer plausible explanations for many of the incidents, the mystery surrounding the unexplained disappearances persists. The region's complex mix of weather patterns, challenging navigation, and a human tendency to seek answers in the supernatural has led to a continuous stream of speculation and investigation.

Ultimately, the truth behind the Bermuda Triangle's mysteries may remain elusive. While science has made strides in understanding the area's natural hazards, some incidents may forever remain unexplained. The Triangle's legacy, however, is secure. It serves as a reminder of the vastness and power of nature, and of the enduring human fascination with the unknown. The mysteries of the deep, like the depths themselves, continue to beckon, inviting us to ponder the unexplainable and the boundless possibilities of the world around us.

The Crooked Forest

Introduction

The Crooked Forest, nestled in a remote corner of Western Poland, is a truly bizarre sight. Here, roughly 400 pine trees, planted around 1930, all curve dramatically northward at their base before straightening out again towards the sky. This strange phenomenon has captivated scientists, nature enthusiasts, and conspiracy theorists alike, leading to a multitude of theories and hypotheses attempting to unravel the mystery of the Crooked Forest.

Theories of Man-Made Manipulation:

One of the most popular theories suggests human intervention is the cause of the trees' peculiar shape. This theory proposes that local farmers or foresters deliberately bent the young trees, perhaps to create uniquely curved timber for furniture or boatbuilding.

This hypothesis is strengthened by the fact that all the trees appear to have been bent in a similar manner at the same age. Furthermore, the curvature seems to occur within the first few years of growth, suggesting a period of deliberate manipulation.

However, specifics about the exact method used to bend the trees are largely speculative. Some believe a tool or weight was used to apply pressure, while others suggest a combination of techniques, perhaps involving ropes and wooden frames.

The Role of Natural Forces:

While human intervention seems a likely culprit, some scientists believe that natural forces could also have played a part in creating the Crooked Forest.

One such hypothesis proposes that a heavy snowfall during the trees' early years could have been responsible. The weight of the snow might have bent the young, flexible trees permanently. Snowfall coupled with prevailing winds from the north could have further contributed to the consistent northward curve observed.

Another potential natural cause could be genetics or a localized environmental factor. It's possible that the trees grew from seeds that carried a unique genetic mutation influencing their growth patterns. Or perhaps, the soil composition, sunlight exposure, or some other environmental influence within that specific area contributed to the unusual shape.

The Influence of Gravity and Growth:

Some theories focus on the unique interaction of gravity and the trees' growth patterns. It's theorized that the trees might have reacted to a stronger gravitational pull in a specific area, influencing their growth trajectory.

Alternatively, a shift in the local magnetic field could have potentially played a role. Magnetic fields can influence the cellular structure and growth of plants, and it's possible that a localized anomaly could have caused the trees to lean in a specific direction. However, these theories are less widely accepted and are mostly considered speculative.

Alien Involvement:

In the realm of the bizarre, some wild theories venture into the territory of extraterrestrial activity. While most scientists dismiss this idea as pseudoscience, it has nonetheless captured the imaginations of many enthusiasts. The idea that aliens could have visited Earth and altered the trees forms part of a broader tapestry of folklore surrounding the Crooked Forest. While one might chuckle at this notion, it does speak to the human penchant for storytelling in the face of the unknown.

The Draw of the Unknown:

What is fascinating about the Crooked Forest is not just the trees themselves, but the way they inspire curiosity and wonder. For visitors, the crooked trees evoke feelings of mystery and intrigue, prompting exploration and discovery. Photographers travel from all corners of the globe to capture the enchantment of this natural oddity, while families and nature enthusiasts find joy in discovering the grove.

Visitors report feelings of awe upon entering the forest, as if stepping into a fairytale—or perhaps another world entirely. The experience of navigating among these peculiar trees often sparks conversations about nature's quirks, and the twisting trunks invite deeper contemplation about the unseen forces that shape our world.

The Limitations of Evidence and the Ongoing Mystery:

Despite the variety of theories, the Crooked Forest remains a mystery. There's limited concrete evidence to conclusively pinpoint a single cause. The absence of historical records from the trees' early years hinders our ability to determine exactly what happened.

Furthermore, the unique circumstances of the Crooked Forest, with its relatively small number of affected trees in a relatively contained area, make it difficult to draw solid conclusions from broader scientific studies on tree growth and development.

Conclusion

The Crooked Forest stands as a testament to the wonders of nature, inviting us to ponder, explore, and dream. While we may not definitively know the causes behind the trees' unique formations, the assortment of theories reflects our deep fascination with the natural world. The magic of the Crooked Forest lies not merely in the unusual shape of its trees, but in our enduring quest to understand the mysteries that nature offers.

Next time you find yourself standing among the crooked trunks, take a moment to immerse yourself in the beauty of uncertainty—a reminder that not all mysteries have to be solved, and that sometimes, the questions are just as valuable as the answers.

Blood Falls

Introduction

Have you ever heard of Blood Falls? It sounds like something from a scary movie, right? But, surprisingly, it's a real place in Antarctica! Located in the McMurdo Dry Valleys, Blood Falls pours out of the Taylor Glacier, and it gets its name from the strange deep red color of the water. Let's dive into the theories and hypotheses that scientists have about this unusual natural wonder.

The discovery of Blood Falls:

The Blood Falls were first discovered in 1911 by the Australian geologist Thomas Griffith Taylor, who was part of the British Antarctic Expedition led by Robert Falcon Scott. Taylor explored the valley that now bears his name and noticed a strange reddish stain on the glacier's snout.

What Are Blood Falls?

Blood Falls is a waterfall that flows from the Taylor Glacier into Lake Bonney. Instead of clear water, it looks like blood, which is why it has such a chilling name. So, how can a waterfall be red? Is it really blood? Let's find out!

A Frozen Time Capsule:

The Taylor Glacier, where Blood Falls originates, is a massive river of ice that has been frozen for millions of years. Trapped beneath it lies an ancient hypersaline lake, a body of water with extremely high salt content. This lake, isolated from the outside world for a long time, has become a unique and fascinating environment.

Theories and Hypotheses:

The reddish color of Blood Falls has been a source of wonder and speculation. Early theories suggested it was due to algae or other microorganisms. However, more detailed research revealed a surprising explanation:

Iron Oxidation: The most accepted theory today is that the red color comes from iron-rich saltwater. The ancient lake trapped beneath the glacier contains high concentrations of iron. When this iron-rich water comes into contact with oxygen in the air, it undergoes a chemical reaction called oxidation. This oxidation process causes the iron to rust, producing the characteristic red color we see in Blood Falls.

Microbial Life: While not the primary cause of the red color, scientists have discovered that specific microbes also play a significant role in the Blood Falls ecosystem. These microbes, adapted to survive in extremely harsh conditions, thrive in the absence of sunlight and use sulfate and iron to produce energy. These microbes may help in the release of the iron that ultimately causes the red colour.

The Role of the Subglacial Lake: The existence of this ancient, isolated subglacial lake is crucial to understanding Blood Falls. It acts as a reservoir of iron and other minerals. The lake's unique composition allows for the survival of unique microbial communities and the continued flow of the iron-rich water that creates Blood Falls.

Why Is Blood Falls Important?

Blood Falls is not just an interesting sight; it is important for science, too! It helps researchers understand how life can exist in extreme conditions.

Conclusion

Blood Falls is a fascinating natural phenomenon that leaves many people curious. While we may have several theories explaining its striking red color, there is still so much to learn. Scientists continue to study this incredible waterfall in Antarctica, revealing secrets about our planet's past and the potential for life in extreme conditions. Next time you think about Blood Falls, remember it's not just a creepy name, it's a window into the mysteries of Earth!

Chapter 3

Paranormal Hotspots

The Winchester Mystery House

Introduction

The Winchester Mystery House, located in San Jose, California, is one of the most intriguing and mysterious buildings in the United States. This massive sprawling Victorian mansion, built in the late 19th century, with its staggering 160 rooms, 2,000 doors, and 47 fireplaces has fascinated visitors and researchers alike due to its unusual architecture and the stories surrounding it. Let's dive into some of the theories and hypotheses that explain why this house is so mysterious.

A Brief History

The mansion was built by Sarah Winchester, who was the widow of William Wirt Winchester, the inventor of the famous rifle. After her husband's death, Sarah inherited a large fortune from the Winchester Repeating Arms Company. She began building the house in 1884. Over the next 38 years, she continued to construct and modify the mansion, driven by a mysterious force that seemed to propel her forward. Many people believe that she started building the house to escape her grief, but others suggest that it was more than that.

The Ghostly Theories:

One of the most popular theories about the Winchester Mystery House is that it was built to appease the spirits of those killed by the Winchester rifle. According to this belief, Sarah Winchester was informed by a psychic that she was being haunted by these restless spirits. To avoid their wrath, she was told to build a house that would never be finished. This idea led to the house's unique features, like staircases that lead to nowhere and doors that open into walls.

The Architect's Vision:

Another theory is that Sarah Winchester wanted to create a masterpiece that reflected her artistic vision. She added rooms, staircases, and odd features for decades, leading to a sprawling building with more than 160 rooms. Some people believe that the house is a representation of her dreams and imagination, showcasing her creativity despite the chaos in her life.

A Symbol of Grief:

Others see the Winchester Mystery House as a symbol of Sarah Winchester's grief. After losing loved ones, her husband and daughter, she may have used the construction of the house to channel her sorrow and keep herself occupied. The continuous building might represent her struggle with loss and her attempt to find peace.

Architectural Curiosity:

The house itself is a wonder of architecture. It includes features like hidden doors, narrow hallways, and unusual layouts. Some experts suggest that Sarah may have wanted to confuse the spirits, while others think she simply wanted to create a unique home. The architectural oddities have led many to study the house as an example of Victorian-era design, blending various styles and influences along the way.

Mystical Beliefs and Numerology:

Another hypothesis is that Sarah Winchester was fascinated with mystical beliefs and numerology. Many rooms in the house reflect the number 13, which is often associated with superstition. For example, there are thirteen bathrooms and thirteen panels in some doors. Some researchers believe that this reflects her desire for spiritual protection against the ghosts she believed haunted her.

The Séance Room:

One of the most fascinating rooms in the house is the Séance Room, where Sarah allegedly held her spiritualist meetings. The room is adorned with symbols and markings, which some believe are connected to her spiritualist beliefs. Others propose that the room was used for more sinister purposes, such as communicating with malevolent entities.

Conclusion

The Winchester Mystery House remains a compelling puzzle filled with theories and possibilities. Was it built to escape grief, as a tribute to the dead, as an artistic endeavor, or due to deep-seated beliefs in the supernatural? Each angle offers a different perspective on why this house is so fascinating.

Visitors continue to flock to the mansion to explore its winding corridors and discover its many secrets. While we may never know the full story, the Winchester Mystery House will forever be a symbol of mystery and curiosity in American history. Each theory adds a layer to the enchanting story of Sarah Winchester and her remarkable creation.

The Catacombs of Paris

Introduction

The Catacombs of Paris, a vast network of underground tunnels and chambers, hold a macabre fascination for visitors and historians alike. These tunnels, stretching for miles beneath the city, are the final resting place for over six millions of Parisians. But beyond the sheer scale of human remains, the Catacombs have also captured the imagination with a wealth of theories and hypotheses surrounding their origins, purpose, and the stories they whisper from the depths.

The Origins: A Growing Problem

Paris, a bustling city, faced a growing issue in the 18th century – overflowing cemeteries. The city's cemeteries, often located in the heart of populated areas, were overflowing, contaminating the water supply and posing serious health risks. The problem became so severe that the authorities had to find a solution, and the solution was born out of necessity - the Catacombs.

The Catacombs were originally limestone quarries that were dug out in the 13th century. As Paris expanded, the quarries became dangerous due to collapsing tunnels. In the late 18th century, city officials decided to use these empty quarries to address a different problem: overflowing cemeteries. This led to the transfer of bones from various cemeteries to the Catacombs, starting in 1786.

The Hypothesis of Necessity:

The most widely accepted hypothesis surrounding the origin of the Catacombs is that they were created out of pure necessity. The decision was made to relocate the bones from the overcrowded cemeteries to the abandoned quarries beneath the city. This monumental task began in 1786, with workers transferring bones from various cemeteries to the subterranean tunnels, meticulously organizing them into ossuaries.

The Theories of Symbolism and Secrecy:

While necessity is the most logical explanation, some theories propose a deeper, symbolic purpose for the Catacombs. Some believe the Catacombs were not just a dumping ground but a deliberate attempt to create a symbolic underworld, a reminder of mortality and the fragility of life.

Theory of a Symbolic Underworld: Some theorists propose the layout of the bones and the overall design of the Catacombs were intended to create a powerful, symbolic experience for visitors. The vastness of the tunnels and the sheer volume of bones could be viewed as a stark reminder of death and the interconnectedness of all life.

Theory of Secret Societies: Another intriguing hypothesis suggests the Catacombs served as a secret meeting place for underground societies or even religious groups. The tunnels offered a hidden and secure space, perfect for clandestine meetings. While no concrete evidence supports this theory, the idea of a hidden world beneath the city has fueled many legends.

The Legends and Mysteries:

The Catacombs have become a fertile ground for legends and mysteries. Stories of secret societies, hidden rooms, and paranormal activity fill the stories of those who explore these dark depths.

The Legend of the Ghostly Monks: One prevalent legend speaks of ghostly monks who haunt the tunnels, a reminder of the long history of the area and the various uses of the quarries before they became a repository for the dead.

The Stories of Hidden Chambers: Whispers of undiscovered chambers and tunnels, containing secrets yet to be uncovered, continue to stir the imaginations of explorers and enthusiasts.

The Catacombs Today:

Today, the Catacombs are a popular tourist destination, offering a glimpse into Paris's dark past. Visitors can walk through a section of the tunnels, witness the impressive ossuaries, and experience a unique atmosphere that blends history, mystery, and a touch of the macabre.

Conclusion

The Catacombs of Paris stand as a testament to the ingenuity and necessity that drove human action in the face of a daunting challenge. The origins of the Catacombs are rooted in the pragmatic need to address a sanitation crisis. However, the symbolism, mystery, and legends surrounding the Catacombs have added a complex layer of intrigue, inviting us to speculate on the deeper meaning behind this vast and haunting underground world. Whether it was a necessary solution, a symbolic creation, or a secret meeting place for hidden societies, the Catacombs continue to fascinate, both for their historical significance and the enduring power of the stories they hold.

Aokigahara Forest

Introduction

Aokigahara Forest, often referred to as the "Sea of Trees," lies at the base of Japan's famous Mount Fuji. While this lush green forest is beautiful and attracts many visitors, it's also known for a much darker reputation. Over the years, Aokigahara has been linked to a high number of suicides, which has led to various theories and hypotheses regarding the phenomenon. In this section, we'll explore some of these ideas in simple language.

The Suicide Forest:

Aokigahara is often referred to as the "Suicide Forest" because it has a high number of people who have taken their lives there. This sad reputation has made the forest a place of tragedy and sorrow. Many believe that the forest has a dark energy that lures people feeling hopeless.

The Legend of the Ubasute:

One of the most enduring theories relates to a historical practice known as "ubasute," where elderly family members were abandoned in the forest to die during times of famine or hardship. This tradition, although not widely practiced in the region, contributed to the forest's association with death and despair.

This act has left an indelible mark on the forest's collective memory, fueling its dark mythology. It is said that the spirits of those abandoned in the forest, their souls tormented by their tragic fate, still linger among the trees.

Many believe that the spirits of those who have died there wander the forest. This idea has made the forest seem spooky to some. Locals say that if you listen closely, you might hear whispers in the trees or see shadows moving. People have shared stories of feeling an eerie presence when walking through the forest, which adds to the legend of it being haunted.

The Spirits of the Forest:

Some myths tell of supernatural beings that inhabit Aokigahara. According to folklore, these spirits, known as Yūrei. Legends of vengeful yūrei haunting Aokigahara Forest further heighten its sinister reputation. According to Japanese folklore, when someone dies by suicide, their soul may transform into a yūrei, a restless spirit trapped in the mortal realm. These malevolent beings are believed to prey on lost souls, luring them deeper into the forest's depths and driving them to contemplate their own demise.

As visitors explore Aokigahara Forest, they can't help but feel the weight of its history and the echoes of the past. The forest becomes a battleground between the living and the departed, a place where the veil between worlds grows thin, and the boundaries of reality blur. The dark history and supernatural legends surrounding Aokigahara Forest serve as a chilling reminder of the fragility of life and the enduring power of myth and folklore.

Cultural Influence:

One of the most significant theories surrounding Aokigahara is its deep connection to Japanese culture. In Japanese tradition, the forest is often seen as a place of mystery and spirituality. It has been the backdrop for numerous stories and legends, including tales about spirits and demons. This cultural backdrop may contribute to why some people feel drawn to the forest in times of despair. They might seek solace in its silence or believe they might find peace among the trees.

Mental Health Awareness:

Another important factor is the issue of mental health. Japan has faced challenges with mental health awareness, and many people suffer in silence. The pressures of society, family expectations, or financial struggles can lead to feelings of hopelessness. Aokigahara, being a place associated with suicide, may draw those who feel lost, as they see it as a secluded spot where they can escape their pain.

The Forest Environment:

Aokigahara is known for its unique environment. Its dense trees, dark paths, and quiet atmosphere create a sense of isolation. Some theorists suggest that this environment can impact one's mood and emotions. The lack of sunlight due to the thick tree cover and the almost eerie silence may enhance feelings of sadness or desperation for those already struggling.

Media Influence:

The portrayal of Aokigahara in movies, books, and media has also played a role in its reputation. Certain films and documentaries highlight the darker side of the forest, increasing public interest. This exposure may inspire some individuals to visit the forest not just as a tourist destination, but also as a place to end their struggles, thinking that their story might be tied to the forest's mysterious identity.

Access and Remoteness:

Aokigahara is easily accessible, making it a convenient location for those contemplating suicide. The remoteness and the paths that seem to lead to nowhere may also attract those looking for solitude. Once in the forest, individuals can easily get lost, both physically and emotionally. This contributes to the forest's sad history as a site where many choose to end their lives.

A Living Memorial:

Within Aokigahara Forest, numerous reminders of those who have taken their lives can be found. Personal belongings, notes, and memorials are scattered throughout the woodland, serving as haunting reminders of the lives lost within its confines. These mementos act as a living memorial, testifying to the deep emotional struggles faced by those who ended their lives in the forest. Visitors often stumble upon abandoned items such as shoes, photographs, or letters, each carrying a poignant narrative of despair. While some objects remain untouched, others are carefully arranged by volunteers who periodically venture into the forest to honor the deceased and offer solace to their grieving families.

Community Response and Awareness:

In response to the troubling reputation of Aokigahara, local authorities and communities have launched several initiatives. They have installed signs in multiple languages offering help and encouraging visitors to reconsider their choices. Counseling services and hotlines have also been made available, reflecting a growing awareness about mental health issues.

Conclusion

Aokigahara Forest is a place of stunning beauty, but it also represents deep sadness for many. Understanding the theories and hypotheses about why this forest has become known as a tragic site can help us approach the topic with compassion and sensitivity. By raising awareness, promoting mental health support, and building community, we can hope to change the narrative surrounding Aokigahara, transforming it into a place of healing and reflection instead of sorrow.

Chapter 4

Lost Cities and Civilization

El Dorado

Introduction

For centuries, the name El Dorado, translates to "The Golden One" in Spanish, has captivated imaginations, whispering tales of a lost city of gold, a mythical kingdom shimmering under the South American sun. But is it merely a legend spun from the threads of ambition and folklore, or was there a kernel of truth hidden within the shimmering story? This journey delves into the fascinating world of El Dorado, exploring the various theories and hypotheses that have sprung up around this enduring enigma.

The Seeds of Legend:

The myth of El Dorado likely emerged from a complex interplay of cultural practices and the insatiable thirst for gold that gripped European explorers in the 16th century. Indigenous tribes, particularly those inhabiting the Colombian Andes, were known for their elaborate rituals involving gold dust and adornment. These rituals, misunderstood and exaggerated through the lens of European greed, fueled the burgeoning legend of a golden king, El Dorado, who was chief of the Muisca tribe in present-day Colombia. According to legends, this chief, upon his coronation, would cover himself in gold dust from head to toe and travel on a raft to the sacred Lake Guatavita in Central Colombia. Surrounded by the four highest priests adorned with feathers, gold crowns and body ornaments, the leader, naked but for a covering of gold dust, would set out to make an offering of gold objects, emeralds and other precious objects to the gods by throwing them into the lake.

The Spanish conquistadors, driven by tales of unimaginable wealth, quickly seized upon this narrative. They believed that a vast and opulent city, ruled by El Dorado, lay hidden somewhere in the heart of the South American jungle. The allure of El Dorado, a land where gold flowed like water, propelled countless expeditions into the unknown, including the likes of Francisco Pizarro and Gonzalo Pizarro in the 16th century, often ended with disastrous consequences.

However, the overwhelming evidence suggests that the focus on a city may have been a misinterpretation. The rituals of the Muisca, while involving gold, were primarily symbolic and spiritual. El Dorado, in this context, represented a concept rather than a physical location. It was a symbol of power, wealth, and spiritual connection to their deities.

The Theories and Hypotheses:

As exploration and research continued, different theories emerged, attempting to reconcile the legend with the realities of the landscape and the indigenous cultures.

The Lake Guatavita Hypothesis:

This theory remains the most popular, linking El Dorado to the sacred lake and the Muisca rituals. It suggests that the ritual of the golden king was a real ceremony, and the lake itself may have been used as a repository for valuable offerings. In the 19th and 20th centuries, treasure hunters have attempted to drain the lake in search of gold, but with little success. Some claim that the Spanish conquistadors had already removed the gold from the lake before the treasure hunters arrived.

The Lost City of Manoa Theory:

One of the most compelling theories is the "Lost City of Gold" hypothesis. Many explorers and archaeologists believe El Dorado refers to an ancient city that was once adorned with gold and jewels. This theory gained momentum in the 16th century when explorers such as Sir Walter Raleigh, who was a leader of an English military and exploratory expedition known as (Raleigh's El Dorado expedition), reported finding evidence of sophisticated civilizations in the Amazon jungle. He pinpointed the location of this city on the shores of Lake Parime, which is now believed to be a mythical lake. Although the lake does not exist, many still believe that the real El Dorado lies somewhere in the Amazon rainforest hidden beneath the dense foliage, waiting to be discovered.

Cuenca, Ecuador:

Some theorize that the real El Dorado was located in the city of Cuenca, Ecuador. They point out that the city's name means "gold" in the indigenous language and that the nearby Cajas National Park has several lakes that could have been the site of the Muisca ritual.

The Myth of Riches:

Another theory posits that El Dorado was never an actual place. Instead, it became a metaphor for the unattainable dreams of wealth and power. Early Spanish colonizers were driven by their greed and desire for gold, leading them to exaggerate stories of El Dorado. This hypothesis suggests that the quest for El Dorado was less about finding a physical location and more about the insatiable human hunger for riches.

Historical Context:

Some researchers believe El Dorado originated from a mix of indigenous practices and European misunderstandings. As Spanish colonizers encountered Native American tribes, they often misinterpreted their customs and stories. The golden offerings made by indigenous people to their gods could have fueled the legends, leading Europeans to inflate the tales of wealth and grandeur.

Geographic Speculation:

The geographic location of El Dorado is another subject of much debate. Some theorists suggest it lies in the Andes mountains, while others argue it could be somewhere in the jungles of the Amazon. In particular, the area around Lake Guatavita is often cited due to its historical significance as a ceremonial site for the Muisca people. The landscape, rich in natural resources, may have contributed to the rumors and legends of hidden treasures.

The Impact on Exploration:

The pursuit of El Dorado had a profound impact on exploration and colonization in South America. Expeditions, driven by tales of grandeur, led to the mapping of unknown territories, increasing European knowledge of the continent's diverse cultures, landscapes, and resources. However, these quests often resulted in the exploitation and devastation of indigenous populations.

The relentless search for gold took a heavy toll, leading to conflict and suffering for native tribes and forever altering their way of life.

Conclusion

Though the quest for El Dorado may have ended in disappointment for many explorers, its legend continues to captivate our imaginations. Whether a lost city, a metaphor for greed, or a misunderstood cultural practice, the story of El Dorado reflects deep human desires for wealth, adventure, and discovery. As we explore the theories surrounding this fabled land, we should remember the impact of these tales on the indigenous people who once thrived in this rich and diverse environment.

In our modern world, El Dorado serves as a reminder of both the allure of ambition and the necessity of understanding the cultural histories that shape our narratives. Whether we view it as a quest for gold or an exploration of human nature, the legend of El Dorado will remain an enduring symbol of the age-old quest for something greater, something that, perhaps, lies not in riches but in the richness of the journey itself.

The Lost City of Z

Introduction

The Amazon rainforest, covering an area of over 5.5 million square kilometers in South America, has been shrouded in mystery for centuries. Its dense foliage and remote location have made it difficult for explorers to delve deep into its heart. One of the most intriguing stories to emerge from the Amazon is that of the Mythical Lost City of Z, a fabled urban civilization hidden deep within the rainforest. This book aims to delve into the various theories and hypotheses surrounding this enigmatic city, tracing its origins, significance, and the numerous attempts to locate it.

The Story of Colonel Fawcett:

The story of the Lost City of Z begins with the British explorer Colonel Percy Fawcett. A renowned adventurer, Fawcett had spent his life exploring the Amazon, studying its geography, and uncovering its many secrets. In 1925, Fawcett embarked on his most ambitious expedition yet - a quest to find the Lost City, which he named "City Z." He believed that city to be a pre-Columbian civilization of great architectural and cultural significance. According to Fawcett, this city was a remnant of an ancient civilization, filled with gold and artifacts of immense value.

Fawcett's fascination with the Amazon began with his mapping expeditions for the Royal Geographic Society. However, his focus shifted when he stumbled upon fragmented legends and ancient artifacts suggesting a sophisticated civilization that predated the Inca and resided deep within the jungle. This sparked a conviction in Fawcett that a lost city, potentially El Dorado itself, existed and was waiting to be rediscovered.

Fawcett's expedition consisted of himself, his son Jack, and his son-in-law Raleigh Rimell. They ventured deep into the Amazon, braving the treacherous terrain and the ever-present danger of disease and wild animals. Fawcett kept meticulous records of their progress, detailing the numerous challenges they faced and the incredible sights they witnessed.

As they progressed deeper into the rainforest, Fawcett became increasingly convinced that they were close to finding the Lost City of Z. In his final letter to his wife, Fawcett wrote of his excitement and anticipation, promising to return soon with tales of their incredible discovery. However, that letter was to be the last anyone would ever hear from Colonel Fawcett and his companions. They vanished without a trace, leaving behind a mystery that would captivate the world for generations to come.

Theories and Hypotheses:

Over the years, many theories and hypotheses have emerged attempting to explain the disappearance of Colonel Fawcett and the existence of the Lost City of Z. Some of the most popular theories include:

The Indigenous People Theory:

One theory suggests that Fawcett and his companions were killed by an indigenous tribe, perhaps in self-defense or as a sacrifice to their gods. This theory gains credibility from the fact that Fawcett had previously encountered hostile tribes in the Amazon, and his journal entries reveal a growing unease about the safety of their expedition.

The Natural Causes Theory:

Another theory proposes that Fawcett and his companions succumbed to natural causes such as disease, starvation, or accidents. The Amazon rainforest is renowned for its treacherous terrain, and the lack of proper supplies and medical care could have easily led to their demise.

The Abduction Theory:

Some researchers believe that Fawcett and his companions may have been abducted by a lost civilization, perhaps the very one they were searching for. This theory suggests that the trio may have stumbled upon the Lost City of Z but were then taken captive, never to be seen again.

The Hoax Theory:

A more conspiracy-driven theory suggests that Fawcett and his companions staged their own disappearance. According to this theory, Fawcett may have intentionally vanished to escape the pressures of fame or to live out the remainder of his life in the Amazon jungle.

The Search for the Lost City of Z:

Colonel Fawcett's disappearance sparked a frenzy of interest in the Lost City of Z, with numerous expeditions being launched to locate the missing explorer and uncover the truth behind his final expedition. Some of the most notable attempts include:

The George Miller Dyott Expedition (1928):

Miller Dyott, a fellow explorer and friend of Fawcett's, led an expedition to locate the missing trio. Although they covered a significant amount of ground, they were unable to find any concrete evidence of Fawcett's whereabouts.

The Roger Rimell Expedition (1934):

Raleigh Rimell's brother, Roger, led an expedition to the Amazon in search of his missing brother and Fawcett. Their expedition ended in tragedy when Roger Rimell contracted malaria and died.

The Vincent Castrucci Expedition (1951):

Castrucci, an American explorer, claimed to have located the remains of Fawcett and his companions in the Amazon. However, his findings were later disputed, and the true identity of the remains remains a mystery.

The David Grann Expedition (2005):

In 2005, journalist David Grann embarked on an expedition to the Amazon, following in Fawcett's footsteps. Although Grann did not find the Lost City of Z, his expedition revealed new insights into the culture and history of the indigenous people of the Amazon.

Theories About the Existence of the Lost City of Z:

Advanced Indigenous Civilizations: One prominent theory is that advanced pre-Columbian civilizations did indeed exist in the Amazon. Archaeologists have uncovered evidence of complex societies, such as the Marajoara and the Tapajós, which suggests that the Amazon was not only inhabited by simple tribes, but also home to sophisticated cultures capable of constructing large cities and intricate societies. Scholars argue that the vast network of rivers provided trade routes, enabling these civilizations to flourish. The Lost City of Z might represent one of these once-lively centers, now hidden beneath the jungle's thick canopy.

Natural Causes: Another hypothesis points to the possibility that natural events could have destroyed any advanced civilization in the region. The rainforest environment is fraught with challenges: floods, droughts, and diseases. A catastrophic event, such as a violent storm or a major drought, may have caused the collapse of a once-thriving society. This theory raises questions about how quickly and completely history can be erased by nature.

Geoglyphs and Earthworks: Advances in technology have revealed geoglyphs—large earthworks that can only be fully appreciated from above—within the Amazon. These structures might be remnants of ancient civilizations and indicate that the region was densely populated with thriving communities. Some researchers believe these geoglyphs could be linked to the Lost City of Z, suggesting that expansive societies could have flourished where Fawcett believed the city to be.

Modern Exploration and Research:

In recent years, interest in the Lost City of Z has sparked renewed exploration in the Amazon basin.

Archaeologists utilize advanced technologies such as Lidar (Light Detection and Ranging) to map the dense forest. These innovations have revealed evidence of ancient roads, settlements, and structures hidden beneath the trees, lending credibility to the idea that the Amazon was once crisscrossed by civilizations.

Moreover, studies of soil composition and ancient agricultural practices indicate that indigenous peoples were adept at manipulating their environment. This indicates that the Amazon could support larger populations than previously assumed, supporting the possibility of the Lost City of Z being rooted in reality.

Conclusion

The story of the Lost City of Z continues to captivate us to this day, with its allure of hidden riches and ancient mysteries. While we may never know the true fate of Colonel Fawcett and his companions, their disappearance has sparked a renewed interest in the Amazon rainforest and its many secrets. The search for the Lost City of Z serves as a reminder of the power of human curiosity and the enduring allure of the unknown. Whether or not the Lost City of Z exists, its legend has already taken its place in the annals of history, inspiring generations of explorers and adventurers to come.

Lemuria: The Lost Continent

Introduction

Lemuria is a hypothetical "lost land" variously located in the Indian and Pacific Oceans. The theory of Lemuria was devised in 1864 by zoologist Philip Lutley Sclater, who suggested that Madagascar and India both shared a common lemur ancestry that could only have come from a sunken continent. Émile Gaffarel linked Lemuria to the idea, then current, that the similarities between the geology of the lands on either side of the Indian Ocean could be explained by straits open between Madagascar and India until the advent of the last ice age. This idea became popular with mystics, theosophists, and some scientists in the late 19th and early 20th centuries, who created and published Lemurian creation myths that bore little resemblance to the original idea.

The idea of Lemuria originated in the early 19th century when the British zoologist Philip Lutley Sclater proposed the name "Lemuria" for this hypothetical lost continent, derived from the Latin word "lemur," referencing the aforementioned primates. He wrote about the odd occurrence of lemur fossils on both India and Madagascar. At that time, zoologists knew that lemurs existed only on the island of Madagascar and yet their fossils had been found in India. As Madagascar and India were not joined by a land bridge at that time, Sclater suggested that there must have been a land bridge connecting them in the distant past. He called this land bridge "Lemuria", naming it after the lemurs.

The theory of Lemuria was also popularized by scientists like Ernst Haeckel and Alfred Wegener, who proposed Gondwana, a "super-continent", in the early 20th century. Alfred Wegener is known as the father of the theory of continental drift. Alfred Wegener and the theory of continental drift also came about in the early 20th century. Wegener and his theory of continental drift showed how all the continents had once been a single land mass.

So Lemuria was either the name given to a single supercontinent that broke up into smaller land masses, Madagascar and India, or to one of the old continents that once existed in the southern hemisphere and had split many millions of years ago, creating the lands of India, Australia and the Islands of the Pacific.

The Break-up of Lemuria:

So how did Lemuria break up and then disappear? Some say it sank, others that it was destroyed by earthquakes, floods, fire from the sky or even a pole shift. Most believe Lemuria was destroyed in a great explosion, the shock of which caused the breakup of the supercontinent into the continents we see today. The explosion is thought to have been caused by the "brass" of Atlantis, a device for harnessing energy, getting out of control.

This is the view of Theosophists and their view originated with Madame Blavatsky and her book "The Secret Doctrine" published in 1888. It is a lot more than just Lemuria; it is about the history of the earth and of all living things. A Sacred History, a story sometimes told in allegory, symbols or parables.

According to Theosophists, Lemuria was a former continent that existed where the Indian Ocean is today. It was the home of the Lemurians who were the third root race, a highly spiritual but simple and peaceful people. They were said to be Stupid and apish, but very intuitive and psychic.

The Lemurians had a highly developed intuitive sense and were able to know the future but didn't really want to change it. They were also sensitive to the energies of the earth. The Lemurians were thought by Theosophists to be gigantic in size, at least 12 feet tall, with white skin and a kind, friendly and docile nature.

The Lemurians were said to have their own way of life, that of a simple agrarian life. They had a simple animist religion and lived in harmony with the earth and nature. The Lemurians lived in symbiosis with the land and the animal life surrounding it. They were said to never kill or eat meat. The Lemurians could only hunt or kill animals out of self-defense.

The Lemurians were thought to be delicate, artistic and peaceful beings. They had thought, they had philosophy but no speech or language. They had no skills of writing or reading. They do not erect city walls, draw lines of belligerent frontiers, or collect fees to build them. They built no places of worship. They were restricted by the fruit of the tree. But they had knowledge of the universe, its beginning and end.

The Lemurians were also healers and had the power to transmit their knowledge. They could grow plants and cures diseases. The Lemurians had a growing power of thought. They knew that they will be reborn. They were wise and kind. The Lemurians were thought to have a hidden civilization. The Lemurians, were said to be still alive today, living underground.

The Destruction of Lemuria:

Lemuria was said to have been destroyed in a great catastrophe. This is the view of Theosophists in general and of Steiner and Bailey. The Lemurians had reached the height of their civilization and had developed a wisdom and a power that was beyond the understanding of most. Similar to Atlantis, they were thought to have had a device for harnessing energy, the "brass", and it got out of control causing massive destruction culminating in the destruction of Lemuria, in a great explosion.

The destruction of Lemuria is also associated with the sinking of Atlantis, which happened 850,000 years ago according to Theosophists. The two events are seen as connected and happening at the same time, or being caused by the same event, the misuse of advanced knowledge. The Atlantis catastrophe was said to have been an instant event, while Lemuria sank slowly.

The Lemurians were said to have had warning of the coming catastrophe. Some Lemurians, who were Adepts and Masters, escaped the destruction of Lemuria. They went to form the "heart" of the Atlantean civilization, according to Theosophists. The Lemurians took the "heart" of Lemuria, the Lemurian race, its wisdom and its knowledge to Atlantis.

The remnants of the Lemurians, the last of them, were said to have ended their life in a new continent, in the Pacific, which was then called Lemuria. From Lemuria, parts of it broke away and formed (eventually) the islands of Polynesia today, Fiji, New Zealand, Hawaii, and Easter Island. This "new" Lemuria also sank and disappeared around 700,000 years ago, again because of another misuse of knowledge and strength. Rapa Nui, which is Easter Island, is a remnant of Lemuria, and was said to be one of its mountain peaks.

The Lemurians and their continent were said to have survived longer than Atlantis because the Lemurians were thought to be far less warlike and aggressive as those of Atlantis. The Lemurians were more spiritual and sought less to expand and conquer as those of Atlantis.

The remnants of Lemuria were said to have arrived in Atlantis from about 1,000,000 to 850,000 years ago. Only a few of the Lemurians survived. The last of the Lemurians was said to have lived in Atlantis and took part in the catastrophe of Atlantis and to have then given the knowledge of Lemuria to the Atlanteans.

Lemuria is part of a series of root races, of which there are seven. Lemuria, in this context, was the third root race, which lived in the third period of the earth's development. It was preceded by the first and second root races and followed by the fourth, fifth, sixth and seventh root races.

The first root race was called the Polarians, the second root race the Hyperboreans, the third root race the Lemurians, the fourth root race the Atlanteans, the fifth root race the Aryans and the sixth and seventh root races still to come. The root races were thought to have different physical characteristics and different degrees of development.

The Lemurians were said to have been the first race of humans to have a physical body, but still with a highly developed spiritual and intuitive sense. They were thought to have been 3rd race, and the Atlanteans were the 4th. The Lemurians were said to have been more spiritual than the Atlanteans.

The left over Lemurians, after the destruction of Lemuria, went on to become the heart of the Atlanteans civilization, with all its wisdom and knowledge. The Atlanteans were thought to have inherited all that could be salvaged from Lemuria, and to have developed it into something new. But the Atlanteans also misused their power and knowledge, leading to their own destruction.

The Atlanteans were said to have been, like the Lemurians, a highly developed race, with great knowledge and wisdom. They were also thought to have been very powerful and to have built a great civilization, but one that was also flawed. The Atlanteans were said to have had contact with the Lemurians and to have been in awe of their wisdom and power.

The Atlanteans were said to have been highly civilized and to have had a great knowledge of the arts and sciences. They were said to have been great builders and to have built great cities. The Atlanteans were also said to have been great navigators and to have sailed all the world's oceans.

The Atlanteans were also said to have been more aggressive and warlike than the Lemurians. The Atlanteans were said to have been great warriors. They were said to have fought great wars, conquering other lands. The Atlanteans were said to have been proud and ambitious. They were said to have sought to expand and conquer.

The Atlanteans were said to have been destroyed in the same way as Lemuria, by the misuse of their knowledge and power. The Atlanteans were said to have used a device called the "brass" - a device for harnessing energy - wrongly, leading to a massive explosion that destroyed Atlantis in an instant. This happened 850,000 years ago, and at the same time as Lemuria sank. The two events were seen as connected and happening at the same time, or being caused by the same event, the misuse of advanced knowledge.

The remnants of the Atlanteans went to form the "heart" of the Aryan race. The Aryans were thought to have inherited all that could be salvaged from Atlantis and to have developed it into something new. The Aryans were the 5th root race and the one that we know today. The Aryans were thought to have been less spiritual than the Lemurians and Atlanteans and more materialistic. They were thought to have been great creators and to have developed language, writing and the arts.

The root races were thought to have lived in different parts of the world. The Lemurians lived in Lemuria, the Atlanteans in Atlantis and the Aryans in the East, in the lands of today's India and the Middle East. The Aryans were said to have been the first race of humans to have lived in a way that is similar to how we live today. They were thought to have been the first to have developed agriculture, to have built cities and to have created laws and institutions. The Aryans were also said to have been great explorers and to have traveled all over the world. They were said to have been the first to have crossed the oceans and to have discovered new lands.

Geological and Archaeological Speculations:

While the Theosophical interpretation leans towards the mystical, some geological and archaeological theories have attempted to ground Lemuria in a more tangible realm. Some researchers have pointed to the existence of submerged landmasses in the Indian Ocean, like the submerged plateau known as the Kerguelen Plateau, as potential remnants of Lemuria.

The existence of ancient megalithic structures on islands like Madagascar and Sri Lanka, as well as the presence of similar cultural motifs, have also been cited as evidence for a shared ancestral culture that could have originated on a lost continent. However, these theories remain largely speculative, with no definitive archaeological evidence linking them directly to Lemuria.

Challenging the Lemurian Hypothesis:

Despite its enduring appeal, the Lemurian hypothesis faces significant scientific challenges. The geological evidence for a vast, sunken continent in the Indian Ocean is scant. Furthermore, the timescale proposed by Theosophy for the existence of Lemuria contradicts established geological timelines. Plate tectonics, the theory that Earth's surface is divided into plates that move and interact, offers a more plausible explanation for the distribution of species and the formation of landmasses.

While the idea of a lost continent is captivating, it's important to distinguish between the mythical and the scientifically plausible. The geological record indicates that significant landmasses have indeed sunk beneath the waves throughout Earth's history, but the evidence for a continent as vast and as advanced as Lemuria remains elusive.

Conclusion

Whether Lemuria existed as a literal continent or not, its legend continues to resonate across cultures and generations. The idea of a lost paradise, a civilization more connected to nature and spirituality, speaks to a deep human longing for a simpler, more harmonious existence.

Lemuria serves as a reminder that humanity's story is vast and complex, filled with mysteries that continue to spark our imagination. Even if the evidence for a physical Lemuria remains scarce, its enduring legacy as a symbol of a lost golden age and a source of spiritual inspiration remains powerful and continues to fuel ongoing discussions and research into the mysteries of our planet's past.

The search for Lemuria might ultimately be a search for something deeper, a reflection of humanity's yearning for connection, understanding, and perhaps even a glimpse into a future where we rediscover harmony with the natural world.

CONCLUSION

As we conclude our journey through the fascinating and mysterious places scattered across our planet, it's clear that Earth holds many wonders beyond our understanding. From the ancient Pyramids of Giza, standing tall for thousands of years, to the eerie silence of Aokigahara Forest in Japan, each site tells a unique story that whispers secrets of the past.

We've marveled at the incredible ingenuity of humans who built Stonehenge and Machu Picchu, left puzzled by their purposes. The enigmatic Easter Island, with its giant stone moai, invites us to ponder the lost traditions of its people. Nature, too, astonishes us, as seen in Poland's Crooked Forest and Antarctica's Blood Falls, showcasing the strange beauty that can arise from both geological phenomena and human imagination.

Adventurous spirits are drawn to places like the Bermuda Triangle, with its tales of vanished ships and planes, while the Winchester Mystery House enthralls with its bewildering architecture and ghostly legends. The Catacombs of Paris reveal eerie layers of history, reminding us of the countless lives that have come before us.

Legends of El Dorado and the Lost City of Z tease our curiosity about treasures yet to be uncovered, while the myth of Lemuria invites us to reflect on the mysteries of lost civilizations.

In exploring these enigmatic locations, we've uncovered not just fascinating sites, but also the boundless human spirit that seeks to understand, discover, and sometimes simply marvel at the mysteries of our world. These places remind us of the stories that intertwine our pasts with our present, inviting us to continue searching for answers and embracing the enigma of existence.

May this book inspire you to venture out into the world and explore these wonders for yourself, or at the very least, to dream of what lies beyond our everyday experiences. The mysteries of our planet are waiting, beckoning adventurous hearts to seek out their truths.